合作

Social Emotional and Multicultural Learning | Non-Fiction Series

Copyright © 2022 by Level Learning, INC. and Washington Yu Ying PCS™
Original and Edited Text Copyright © 2022 by Washington Yu Ying PCS™

All rights reserved. No part of this book in whole or part may be reproduced without written permission from the publisher.

Published by Level Learning, INC.

Content Contributors:
Washington Yu Ying PCS™
Level Learning - Ya-Ching Chang

Illustrations by: Josh Taira

Leveling classification based on Level Learning standard. For full description, visit www.levellearning.com

ISBN 978-1-64040-086-3
Simplified Chinese Edition

About Level Learning:

Level Learning provides a literacy focused curriculum specifically designed for K-12 Chinese as a Second Language classrooms. Our program offers 20 levels of specific and detailed objectives, leveled texts and passages, mastery-based online assessment, and analytics to enable data-driven instruction. Level Learning reading curriculum for both literature and informational text emphasize grammar and comprehension skills to help teachers develop confident and independent Chinese language readers. The non-fiction series of books are specifically designed to support our informational text course based on multiple national standards. To learn more about our entire offering, visit www.levellearning.com.

About Washington Yu Ying PCS™:

Washington Yu Ying PCS is a Mandarin English dual language immersion International Baccalaureate (IB) World school. Yu Ying's mission is to inspire and prepare young people to create a better world by challenging them to reach their full potential in a nurturing Chinese/English educational environment. Yu Ying's comprehensive IB, dual immersion curriculum equips students with global competencies for success in the real world. As a leader in immersion education, Yu Ying is determined to advance Chinese language programs and global citizenry education by helping other schools create and strengthen their Chinese programs. For more information, email: products@washingtonyuying.org

人们常说:"团结就是力量。"这句话是什么意思呢?这句话告诉我们:大家互相合作,共同完成一件事情,会比一个人做更省时、省力;或者有的时候,有些事情一个人很难完成,只有大家互相合作才能完成。

生活中有许多合作的例子,比如制作一个模型。

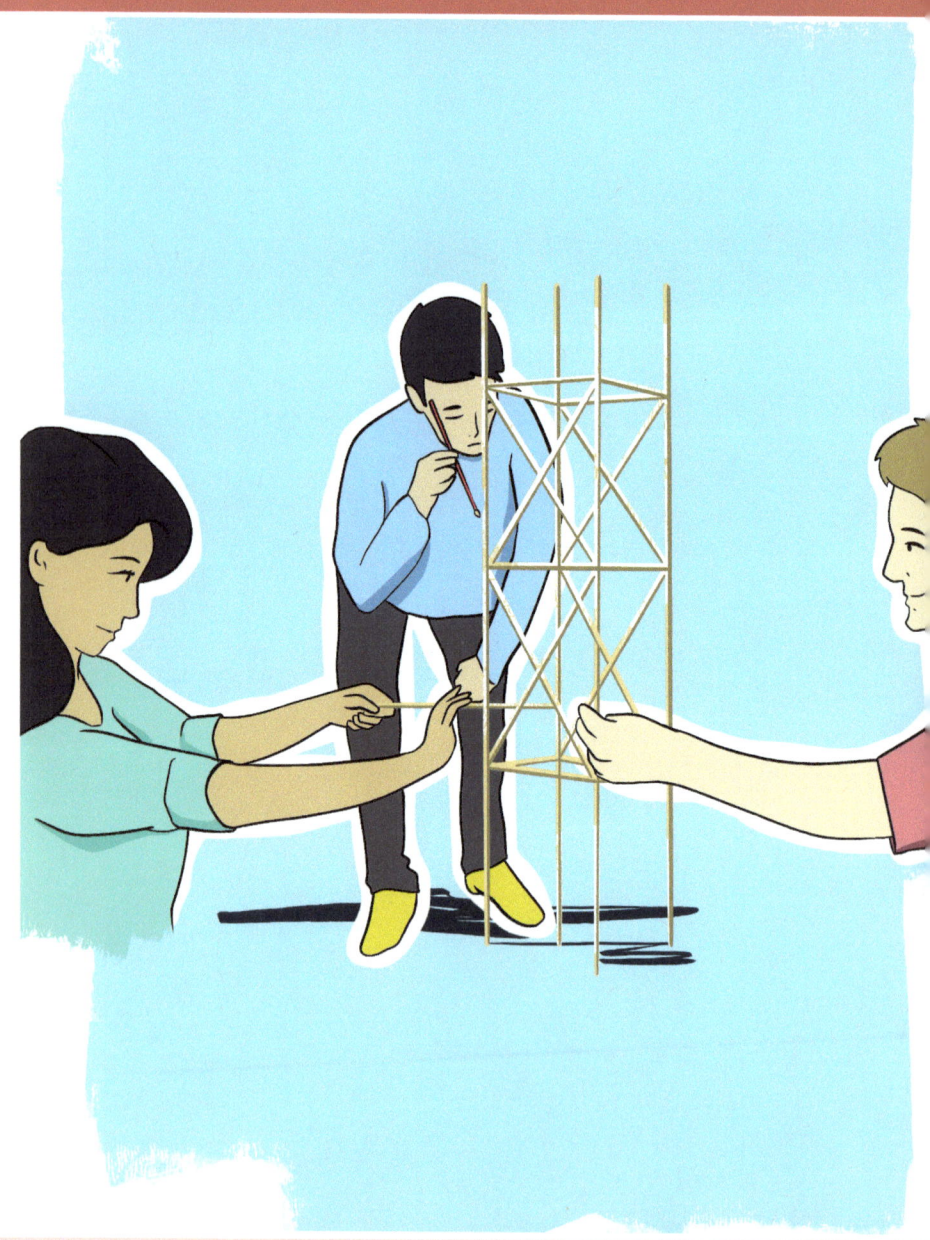

首先，大家一起讨论要制作一个什么样的模型。然后，有的同学负责找材料；有的同学负责把材料处理成可用的形状；有的同学负责涂色等等。最后，通过合作，大家一起完成这个模型。

在这个过程中，每个人都有自己的工作和责任。通过沟通，大家互相帮助，互相支持，才能达到共同的目标。

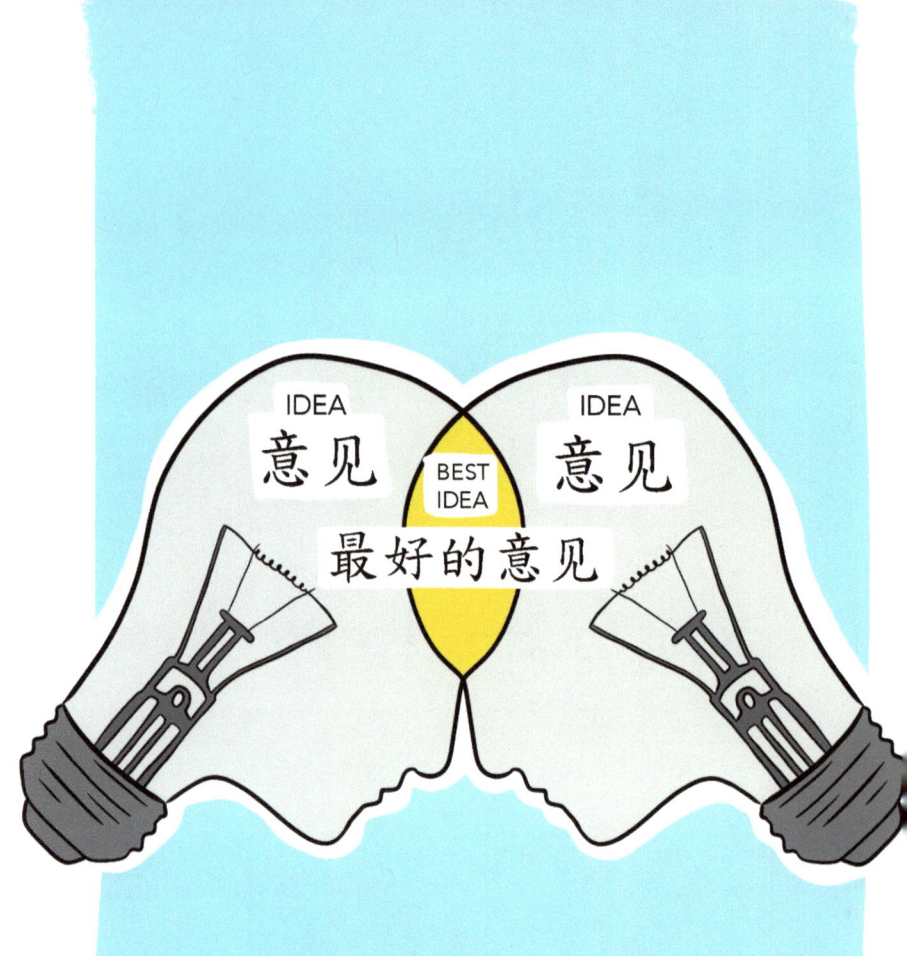

互相合作除了让我们工作省时、省力之外,还为我们带来许多好处。比如说,通过合作,我们可以提高沟通能力,学会清楚地表达自己的想法。同时,我们也可以学习和不同的人合作,学会倾听不同的意见和看法。

另外，在合作过程中，也能提高我们的领导能力。每个组员都有机会负责工作中的一部分。有了正确的领导，每个人都能发挥自己的长处，才能把工作完成得又快又好。

在学校里，我们有许多互相合作的机会，最常见的就是小组报告。在准备报告的过程中，大家一起讨论报告的内容。然后，有人负责在电脑上打出报告的内容，有人负责画图，有人负责上台报告。我们互相合作、互相学习，大家共同进步。

除此之外，和同学一起讨论作业，加入社团活动，做社区服务，都是互相合作的好机会。

合作会为我们带来许多好处。

有机会你也可以试试!

Glossary

	Pinyin	English Definition
团结	tuán jié	united
力量	lì liàng	power
互相	hù xiāng	each other, mutual
合作	hé zuò	collaboration
共同	gòng tóng	jointly, together
完成	wán chéng	to complete, to accomplish
省	shěng	to save, to economize
例子	lì zi	example
制作	zhì zuò	to make
模型	mó xíng	model
讨论	tǎo lùn	to discuss
负责	fù zé	to be responsible
找	zhǎo	to find
材料	cái liào	material
处理	chǔ lǐ	to handle

	Pinyin	English Definition
形状	xíng zhuàng	shape
涂色	tú sè	coloring
完成	wán chéng	to complete
责任	zé rèn	responsibility
沟通	gōu tōng	to communicate
支持	zhī chí	to support
达到	dá dào	to achieve
目标	mù biāo	goal
提高	tí gāo	to increase
能力	néng lì	ability
清楚	qīng chu	to be clear about
表达	biǎo dá	to express
想法	xiǎng fǎ	way of thinking
倾听	qīng tīng	to listen carefully
领导	lǐng dǎo	leadership

Glossary

	Pinyin	English Definition
组员	zǔ yuán	member
机会	jī huì	opportunity
发挥	fā huī	to develop
长处	cháng chù	strong points
小组	xiǎo zǔ	small group
报告	bào gào	report
准备	zhǔn bèi	to prepare
作业	zuò yè	homework
社团	shè tuán	community
活动	huó dòng	activity
服务	fú wù	service

www.ingramcontent.com/pod-product-compliance
Lightning Source LLC
Chambersburg PA
CBHW041221070526
44584CB00001B/41